Understanding
THE LIFE OF JESUS

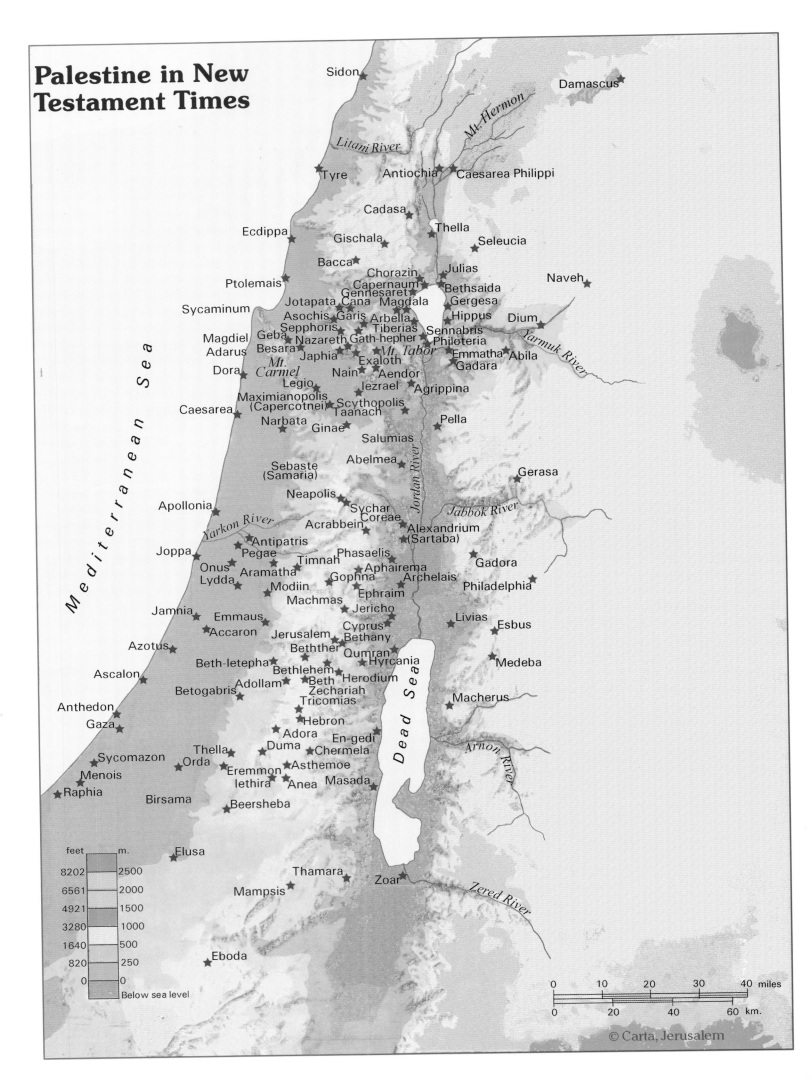

Understanding the LIFE of JESUS

An Introductory Atlas

MICHAEL AVI-YONAH

Revised and Updated by

R. STEVEN NOTLEY

cartaJerusalem

First published in 2015 by
CARTA Jerusalem

Copyright © 2015
Carta Jerusalem, Ltd.
11 Rivka, P.O.B. 2500,
Jerusalem 9102401, Israel
E-mail: carta@carta.co.il
www.carta-jerusalem.com

Editor: Lorraine Kessel
Cartography: Carta, Jerusalem

Excerpted and adapted from: **The Carta Bible Atlas**
Supplies to the Temple and the Bringing of the Omer: Adapted from:
    Carta's Atlas of the Period of the Second Temple;
    the Mishnah and the Talmud; M. Avi-Yonah, S. Safrai
Frontispiece: Adapted from **The Bible Atlas, Carta, Jerusalem**

Great care has been taken to establish sources of illustrations. If inadvertently we failed to do so, due credit will be given in the next
edition.

ISBN: 978-965-220-873-6

Printed in Israel

Table of Contents

FOREWORD

Understanding the land of Jesus is a necessary component to comprehending the message he proclaimed. From the beginning of the four Gospels until their end, the Evangelists assume that we possess an intimate knowledge of the historical and geographical stage onto which Jesus stepped. For most Christian readers this is unfortunately not true. Many have not had the opportunity to visit the Holy Land. Even for those who have, it can prove to be a confusing experience. Much about life in this land has changed over the course of two millennia.

Happily, however, the contours of the land, which influenced where people settled and the routes they travelled, have remained the same. With some basic knowledge of the physical settings we can once again trace Jesus' steps. For example, although the modern roads may not always follow precisely the ancient routes, one must still travel from Nazareth "down to Capernaum" (*Luke 4:31; John 2:12*).

The fruit of a century of archaeological discovery in the Holy Land has also shed important light on the biblical story. The locations of the Galilean cities mentioned in the Scriptures, many of which had been abandoned and lost in time, have been uncovered and identified through the tireless efforts of the archaeologist's spade. In the most recent developments, the new excavation at Magdala, nestled on the edge of the plain of Gennesaret and the northwestern shore of the Sea of Galilee, is a cause for celebration. We can now visit a first-century Galilean synagogue in a harbor city we know Jesus visited by boat on more than one occasion. When we couple the unearthing of Magdala's harbor with the nearby discovery of a sunken first-century boat, we begin to get a clearer picture of life around the lake from the days of the New Testament – a picture whose details were not fully grasped even a generation ago.

It is hoped that these maps and the brief texts that accompany them can serve as a guide for the Christian reader to navigate the geographical stage in the Gospel accounts. Both the maps and the texts have been updated from Avi-Yonah's earlier rich contribution. New discoveries sometimes bring the need for a fresh understanding of the interplay between land and Scripture. May the readers be aided in their pursuit to follow the steps of the Master and to grasp more clearly the message he preached.

R. Steven Notley; Ph.D
Nyack College, NYC

Sea of Galilee with the Golan Heights in the background.
Picture Author: Grandmaster

The Roman Empire & Jewish Diaspora in the Time of Jesus

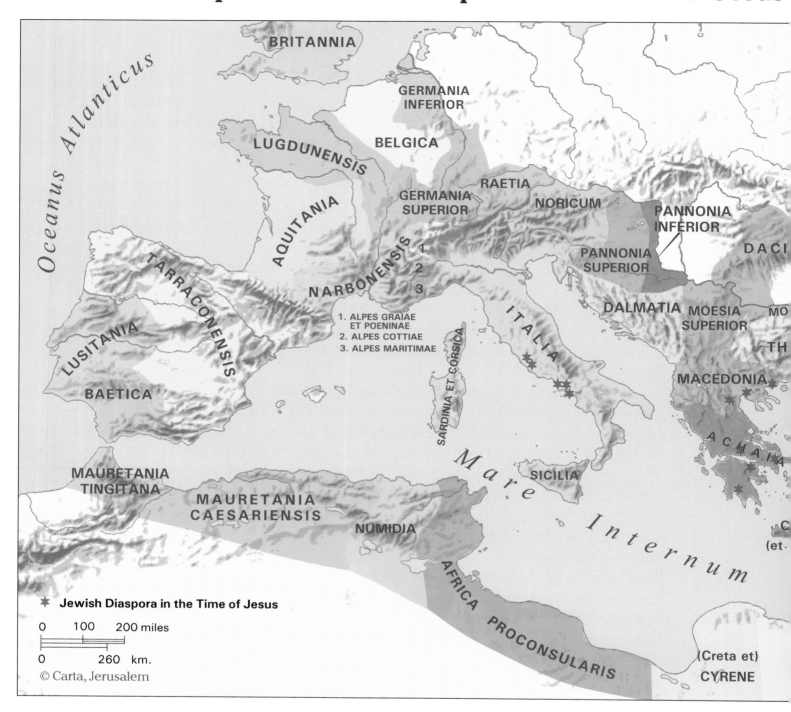

Jewish Diaspora in the Time of Jesus

0   100   200 miles

0   260 km.

© Carta, Jerusalem

At the beginning of the Christian era, the Jewish communities were mainly concentrated in the Eastern, Greek-speaking half of the Roman Empire. Two outlying areas were central Italy, where Jews had been brought as slaves after Pompey's campaign and where conditions became favorable under Julius Caesar, and Babylonia, where the communities grew strong under Parthian rule. But the bulk of the Jewish diaspora was still confined to the Greek world; the largest and most affluent community was in Egypt. There the Jewish communities were centered around the synagogue, with full internal autonomy, their own archons and elders, communicating with each other and with Jerusalem. This state of affairs goes far to explain the context of Paul's missionary activity. The communities were on the whole prosperous, but dependent on Gentile authorities and anxious to preserve good relations with them. The Jewish diaspora was linked to Jerusalem by strong religious bonds; as long as the Temple stood, thousands of pilgrims came every year from outlying communities to fulfill the duty of "going up to the mountain of the Lord" on one of the three main festivals. The collection of the Temple tax in the Jewish Diaspora, and the transport of this offering, was protected by the Roman government. Every adult male Jews was expected to contribute. This even more than pilgrimage maintained the cohesiveness of the Jewish world centered around the Temple.

At these times Jerusalem assumed a strangely cosmopolitan air,

> Now there were dwelling in Jerusalem Jews, devout men every nation under heaven.
>
> *(Acts 2:5)*

4. PHRYGIA PARORIEUS
5. ISAURIA
6. LYCAONIA

Coin of Herod Antipas, struck at Tiberias (Carta, Jerusalem)

1 MACC. 15:23; ACTS 2:8-11; ANT. 14:213-264; PAPYRI; INSCRIPTIONS

Ancient merchant ship represented on a sarcophagus from Sidon (Carta, Jerusslem)

the western diaspora; Crete and Arabia (the "Nabatene") round off his survey. The variety of coins found in Jerusalem from the late Second Temple period testifies to the extensive trade carried on between Jerusalem and various countries.

people from West and East jostling one another, speaking a rich variety of languages. According to the story as told in Acts, many of the pilgrims came to hear the Apostles and were astounded to be addressed in their own languages. On this occasion, the author of Acts gives (Acts 2:9-10) an extensive survey of the diaspora of his time (which possibly looks back symbolically to the tower of Babel and the giving of the Law), beginning with the East, which was beyond the boundaries of the Roman Empire — Parthia, Media, Elam, and Mesopotamia. He then gives Judea and, going north, lists Cappadocia and Pontus; from the shores of the Black Sea he turns westward to the province of Asia, then inland to Phrygia and Pamphylia. From there he moves on across the sea to Egypt and its neighbor, Cyrene. Rome, with its Jews and proselytes, represents

Reconstruction of Herod's Temple in Jerusalem, center of Jewish worship in the Second Temple Period. (Photo: Edmund N. Gall)

9

The Growth of Herod's Kingdom - 40 to 4 B.C.

The thought could not but occur both to Caesar himself and to his soldiers that Herod's realm was far too restricted, in comparison with the services which he had rendered them.

(War 1:396)

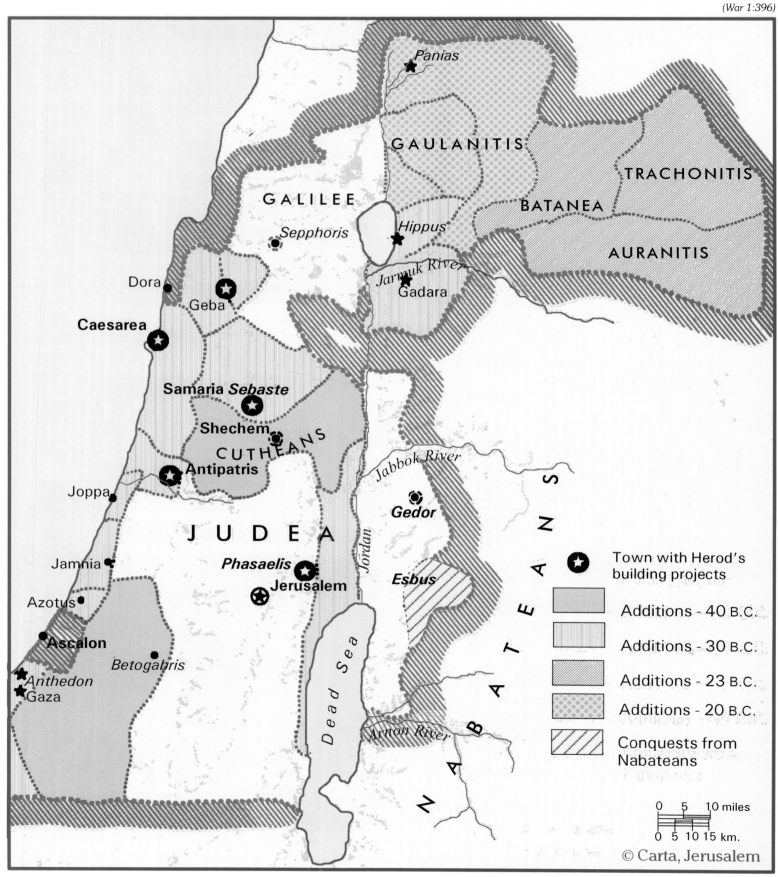

Panias

GAULANITIS

TRACHONITIS

GALILEE

BATANEA

Sepphoris

Hippus

AURANITIS

Jarmuk River

Dora

Gadara

Geba

Caesarea

Samaria *Sebaste*

Shechem

CUTHEANS

Jabbok River

Antipatris

Joppa

Gedor

JUDEA

Jordan

Jamnia

Phasaelis

Esbus

Jerusalem

Azotus

Ascalon

Betogabris

Dead Sea

N A B A T E A N S

Anthedon

Gaza

Arnon River

Town with Herod's building projects

Additions - 40 B.C.

Additions - 30 B.C.

Additions - 23 B.C.

Additions - 20 B.C.

Conquests from Nabateans

0   5   10 miles

0 5 10 15 km.

© Carta, Jerusalem

ANT. 15:217, 343, 344, 360; WAR 1:396, 398, 400; APPIAN: CIVIL WARS 5:75

The Herodium
Photo: Asaf T.

Bronze coin of Herod the Great
minted at Samaria
Author: PHGCOM; Photographed at the
British Museum

Herod maintained his position under Cleopatra, and when the battle of Actium (31 B.C.) made Octavian — now the emperor Augustus — undisputed master of the Roman world, Herod quickly gained the favor of his new overlord. He was confirmed in his kingdom, to which Augustus in 30 B.C. added Gaza and the coastal cities (except Ascalon and Dora) as well as Gadara and Hippus.

In 23 B.C., Herod received the task of pacifying the unruly Batanea, Trachonitis, and Auranitis, and in 20 B.C., Panias and Gaulanitis were placed under his rule. By then Herod's kingdom had reached its greatest extent.

Apart from the conquest of his own kingdom, Herod made only one conquest by arms: having in 32 B.C. defeated the Nabateans in the field, he annexed Esbus and settled veterans there.

A view of Herod's Temple and the surrounding city in the days of Herod.
Holyland Model of Jerusalem
(Photo: Berthold Werner)

The Economy of Palestine at the Time of Jesus
Fourth Century B.C. to First Century A.D.

Well, ours is not a maritime country: neither commerce ... We devote ourselves to the cutivation of the productive country with which we are blessed.

(Against Apion 1:60)

Thanks to its agricultural wealth, Judea was prosperous in the days of the Second Temple, a prosperity that began with the Hellenistic period mainly during the reign of Janneus. The areas suitable for wheat-growing were indeed few, and their extent limited: the Esdraelon Valley, parts of the coastal plain and some of the larger mountain valleys. In the south, barley took the place of wheat. Olives and vineyards thrived in the mountains. Dates were grown mainly in the hot Jordan Valley and balsam on the royal estate near Jericho. Wool from the mountains of southern Judea served to clothe the population. The western slopes of the mountains, on both sides of the Jordan, were still covered with extensive forests, and a good part of the Sharon was wooded with oaks. These regions also served as pasture lands for sheep and cattle.

Various industries connected with the Temple and life in the metropolis in general existed in Jerusalem. Pottery, tied as it was to sources of raw material, was probably the country's one major industry; the others (mainly spinning and weaving) were home industries. Fishing boats plied the Sea of Galilee and the Mediterranean, and murex shells yielding purple were collected and processed at Azotus, Dora, and farther north.

The name Taricheae, "place of salted fish," is evidence of a fish-preserving industry, which probably exported its produce. Copper from the Arabah, iron from the mountains of Gilead, and bitumen from the Dead Sea were the main natural resources; to these must be added the hot springs at Callirrhoe and Baaras as well as those near Pella, Gadara, and Tiberias.

Israelite scouts returning with bunch of grapes of Canaan;
(Numbers 13:23)
(Museum Rotterdam)

Coin of Herod Antipas: 4 BCE-39 CE.
Dated year 34 (30 CE); showing palm branch.
(Classical Numismatic Group, Inc).

KEY TO ECONOMY OF JUDEA

Wine	Cattle
Peas	Sheep
Figs	Goats
Nuts	Asses
Pomegranates	Hounds
Persimmons	Wheat
Dates	Forests
Pottery	Olives
Tyrian purple	Barley
Hot springs	Gardens
Iron	Glass Sand
Fishing	Port
Camels	Small harbor
Horses	

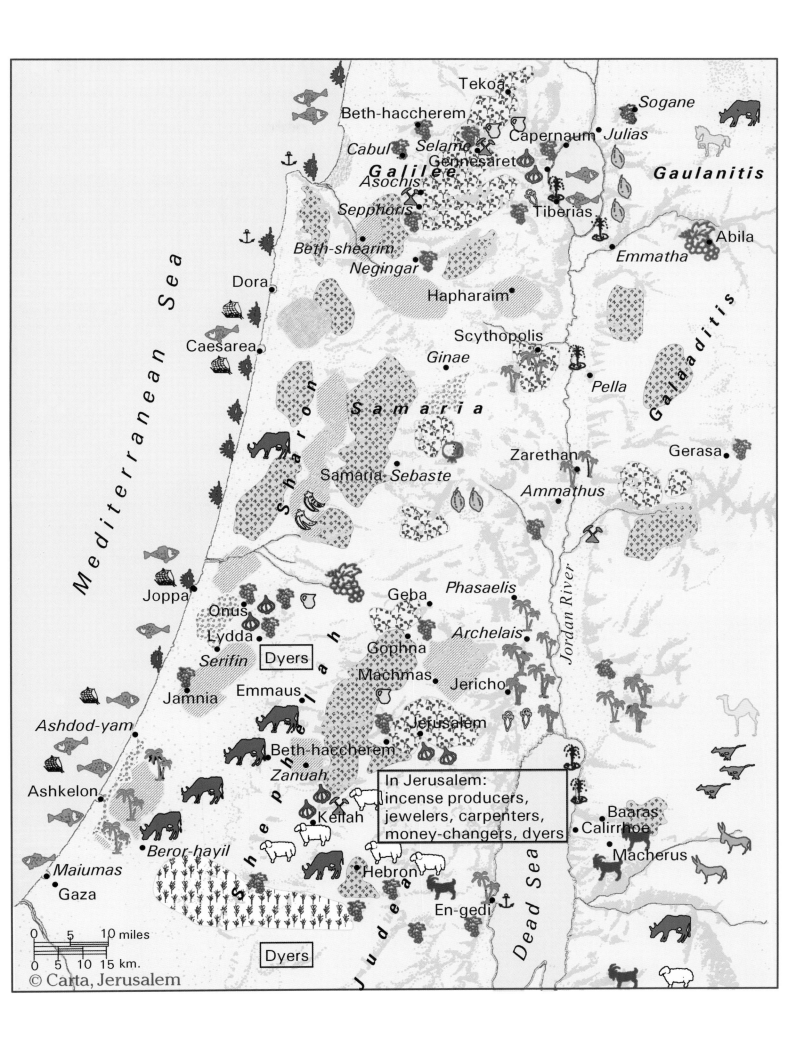

Tekoa

Beth-haccherem

Sogane

Cabul   *Selame*

Capernaum   *Julias*

Gaulanitis

Asochis   Gennesaret

Galilee

Sepphoris   Tiberias

Abila

Emmatha

Beth-shearim

Dora

Negingar

Hapharaim

Galaaditis

Scythopolis

Caesarea

Ginae

Samaria

S a m a r i a

Pella

Zarethan

Gerasa

Samaria-*Sebaste*

Ammathus

S h a r o n

Joppa

Geba   *Phasaelis*

Onus

Archelais

Lydda

Gophna

Dyers

Serifin

Machmas

Jericho

Emmaus

Jamnia

S h e p h e l a h

Jerusalem

Ashdod-yam

Beth-haccherem

Zanuah

In Jerusalem:
incense producers,
jewelers, carpenters,
money-changers, dyers

Ashkelon

Baaras

Keilah

Calirrhoe

Beror-hayil

Macherus

Maiumas

Hebron

J u d e a

Gaza

En-gedi

Dead Sea

M e d i t e r r a n e a n   S e a

Jordan River

0 5   10 miles

0 5   10 15 km.

© Carta, Jerusalem

Dyers

13

Supplies to the Temple and the Bringing of the Omer

The Temple service with its wide variety of sacrifices mandated a steady supply of agricultural produce and livestock brought to Jerusalem from outside its confines. The Halacha and consequent practice required that all goods destined for the Temple were to be of the finest quality. Therefore, we find listed in the sources mainly in Massechet Menachot in the Mishnah and the Tosefta lists of places that had superior produce and were therefore the preferred sources of requirements for the altar. The sources of produce were not limited to Jerusalem or Judea but were chosen from all parts of the country wherever Jews resided.

The most important goods mentioned in the sources are (1) fine flour; wheat products – the best of which grew in Michmas and Zanoah in Judea. These two locations produced "Alpha" fine flour (semolina). Second to these was Hapharaim in the Beisan Valley. (2) The fine oil from Tekoa (in Galilee), Regev in Transjordan, and Gush Halav in Galilee. (3) The best wine came from Tolim, (a place unidentified) and Kruchim in the Jordan Valley. Wine of a lesser quality came from Beth-rima and Beth-laban in Judea and from Sogane in Galillee. Other sources tell of the supply of sheep from the desert, deer from Moab, fledgling birds from Har Hamelech, and calves from the Sharon.

Bringing the Omer of barley on the first day of Pessah was a gift of the year's first grain and was accompanied by much attention and joy. The Mishnah states that the Omer should come from near Jerusalem, and great efforts were made in order to bring it from as close as possible to Jerusalem "Mitzvat Ha'omer to come from nearby". However, it was not always the first to ripen, or even be in season. In such cases, the Omer was brought from wherever it ripened first. The Mishnah relates that at one time the Omer was brought from Gannot Tserifin, and the two loaves from the valley of En Socher near to Shechem.

Prutah coin of the Kings of Judea,. 6 C.E. bearing three ears of barley.
Attribution: Classical Numismatic Group, Inc.

Barley field
(Author: Rastrojo)

"Ye shall bring out of your habitations two wave loaves of two tenth deals: they shall be of fine flour; they shall be baken with leaven; they are the firstfruits unto the Lord."
Lev 23:17

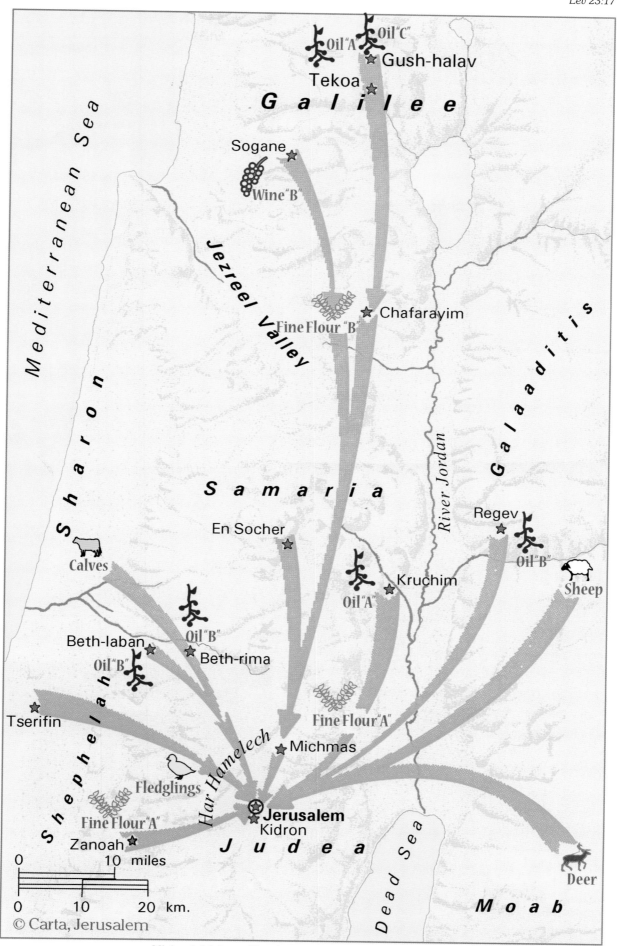

Mishnah Ma'aser Sheni 85, 2; Mishnah Menahot 88, 1, 2, 6; Tosefta Menahot 85, 5.

15

The Birth of Jesus and the Flight into Egypt

And she gave birth to her first-born son ... and laid him in a manger, because there was no place for them in the inn.

(Luke 2:7)

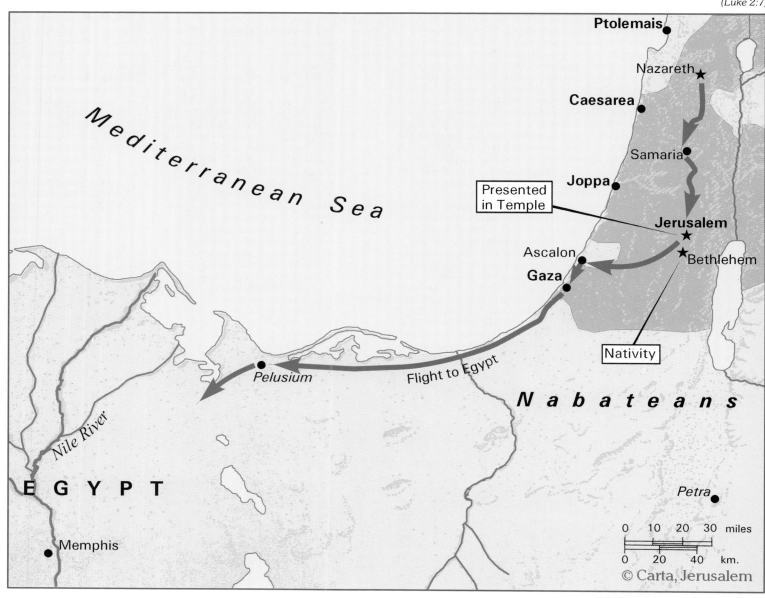

MT 1:18-2:15; LK. 2:4-38

The story of Jesus is set out in the four gospels of Matthew, Mark, Luke, and John. The first three are called the "synoptic" gospels, because they are studied together owing to their similarity; the fourth gospel, that of John, contains many details not found in the others and is different in many other ways also.

According to Christian tradition, Jesus was born at Bethlehem in the days of King Herod (who died in the spring of 4 B.C.); Jesus' birth probably occurred in December, 5 B.C. According to Luke (2:22-24), the child was presented at the Temple. Menaced by Herod, Joseph and Mary decided to flee to Egypt by night. The shortest way to leave Herod's domain was seemingly by way of Ascalon, which lay on the main route to Egypt; the safer way of the desert would have been too arduous for a woman and a newborn babe. The family arrived unharmed in the land of the Nile, where they found shelter and sustenance among the many Jews then living in Egypt..

Bethlehem, Grotto of the Nativity
(Photo: Abraham)

The Return From Egypt; The Boy Jesus in the Temple

After the death of Herod, Joseph had a vision in which he was warned not to return to the environs of Jerusalem. Archelaus, the son of Herod, now ruled in Judea; and he exceeded his father's tyranny.

Instead, Joseph settled in Nazareth, a small Jewish village about seven miles southeast of Sepphoris, the capital of western Galilee. Scant attention is given to Joseph's likely geopolitical reason for choosing Nazareth. The remote village lay in territory under the milder rule of Herod Antipas and beyond the murderous reach of Archelaus.

The traditional route of return along the coast takes little account of the warning to avoid the territory of Archelaus. While Matthew does not specify, Joseph may have circumvented these districts and followed the well-known southern route from Rhinocorura at the Brook of Egypt towards Petra. Their journey north beyond the Jordan would then have passed through Perea and approached Nazareth in Galilee from the southeast.

View of Nazareth today
(Photo: Fares)

And Jesus increased in wisdom and in stature
and in favor with God and man.
(Luke 2:52)

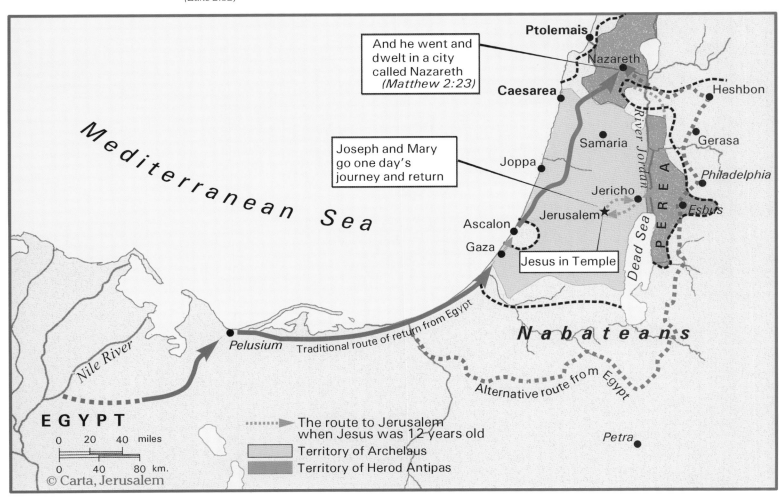

And he went and dwelt in a city called Nazareth *(Matthew 2:23)*

Joseph and Mary go one day's journey and return

Jesus in Temple

Traditional route of return from Egypt

Alternative route from Egypt

EGYPT

0 20 40 miles
0 40 80 km.
© Carta, Jerusalem

⋯⋯> The route to Jerusalem when Jesus was 12 years old
▨ Territory of Archelaus
▨ Territory of Herod Antipas

The Baptism of Jesus and the Sojourn in the Desert

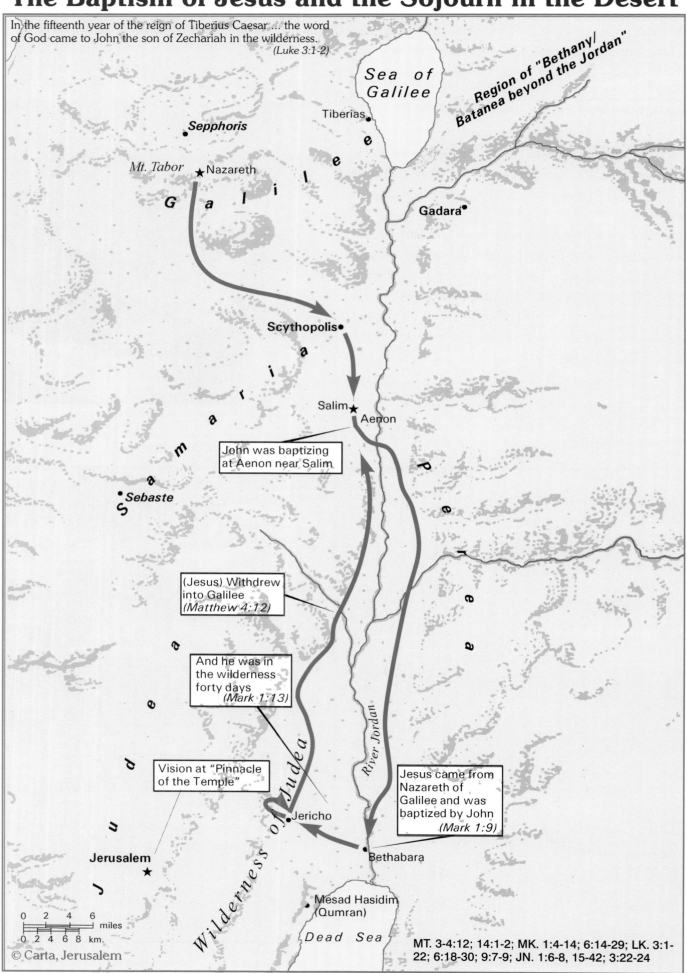

In the fifteenth year of the reign of Tiberius Caesar ... the word of God came to John the son of Zechariah in the wilderness.
(Luke 3:1-2)

Sea of Galilee

Region of "Bethany/Batanea beyond the Jordan"

Tiberias

Sepphoris

Mt. Tabor ★ Nazareth

Gadara

G a l i l e e

Scythopolis

S a m a r i a

Salim ★ Aenon

John was baptizing at Aenon near Salim

Sebaste

P e r e a

(Jesus) Withdrew into Galilee *(Matthew 4:12)*

And he was in the wilderness forty days *(Mark 1:13)*

River Jordan

Vision at "Pinnacle of the Temple"

Jesus came from Nazareth of Galilee and was baptized by John *(Mark 1:9)*

J u d e a

Wilderness of Judea

Jericho

Bethabara

Jerusalem ★

Mesad Hasidim (Qumran)

0 2 4 6 miles
0 2 4 6 8 km.
© Carta, Jerusalem

Dead Sea

MT. 3-4:12; 14:1-2; MK. 1:4-14; 6:14-29; LK. 3:1-22; 6:18-30; 9:7-9; JN. 1:6-8, 15-42; 3:22-24

18

Statue of the emperor Augustus in Museo Chiaramonti,
Vatican, Rome
(Photo: Till Niermann)

The beginning of Jesus' public activity, the "fifteenth year of the reign of Tiberius Caesar" (that is, A.D. 27-28), was also when John the Baptist began to preach "a baptism of repentance for the forgiveness of sins" (Luke 3:1-3). Combining the Gospel story with other historical sources of the period (in particular Josephus and the Qumran documents), we see the activity of John as part of a deep spiritual ferment pervading the whole of Judea at that time. John's activity was concentrated in the "region about the Jordan" (Luke 3:3), possibly at the traditional site of Bethabara at the fords of the Jordan near Jericho, or higher up the river at Aenon (identified in the fourth century as lying two miles south of Salim; today Khirbet ed-Dir, south of Scythopolis (Beth-shean). Recently a proposal has been advanced that "Bethany beyond the Jordan" instead represents the Greek "Batanea beyond the Jordan" in the region north of the Sea of Galilee which is also a region where the Jordan River flows. Among the multitudes who flocked to be baptized was Jesus, who came from Nazareth in Galilee. This was the beginning of his ministry.

According to the Gospels, his baptism was followed by forty days of seclusion in the wilderness, most probably the wilderness of Judea. The wilderness has from time immemorial been a refuge for those who have wished to isolate themselves from the world. The sequence of baptism and seclusion in the wilderness was common at the time. Gospel tradition has it that Jesus was tempted by Satan in the wilderness and led by the evil spirit to the "pinnacle of the Temple" in Jerusalem — presumably the southeastern corner of the Temple Mount — which had a sheer drop of 130 feet. Having overcome temptation, Jesus returned to Galilee. John continued to preach and baptize and was ultimately arrested by order of Herod Antipas (Mark 6:14-29; Matthew 14:1-12; Luke 3:19-20.

Judean Wilderness.
(Photo: Julien Menichin)i

From Nazareth to Cana and Capernaum

Follow me and I will make you become fishers of men.
(Mark 1:17)

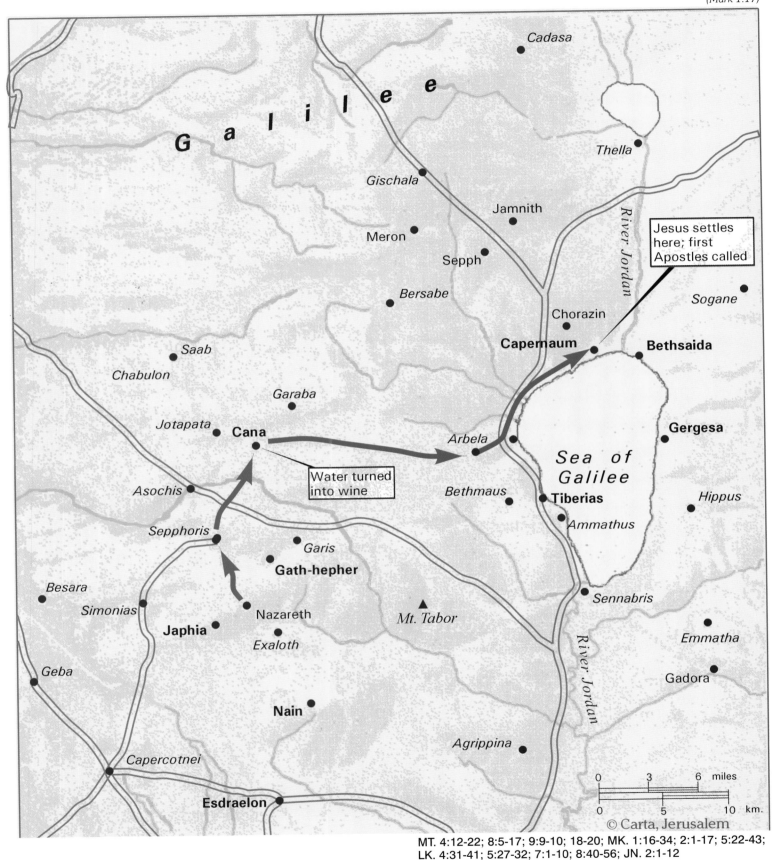

MT. 4:12-22; 8:5-17; 9:9-10; 18-20; MK. 1:16-34; 2:1-17; 5:22-43;
LK. 4:31-41; 5:27-32; 7:1-10; 8:40-56; JN. 2:1-12

According to Luke 3:23, Jesus was about thirty years old when he began his ministry. The evangelist records that at the beginning Jesus visited the synagogue of his childhood village of Nazareth (Luke 4:16-30). Mark (6:1-6), on the other hand, inserts the episode later within the context of Jesus' teaching around the Sea of Galilee. In Matthew 13:53-58 the event is placed in the same context, and Jesus is here called the "carpenter's son." Through his public reading in Nazareth's synagogue of a creative combination of

From Nazareth to Nain

And it came to pass the day after, that he went into a city called Nain; and many of his disciples went with him, Now when he came nigh to the gate of the city, behold, there was a dead man carried out, the only son of his mother, and she was a widow
(Luke 7:11-12)

biblical passages from Isaiah 61:1-2 and 58:6, Jesus challenged their expectations for divine redemption. The audience refused to accept this new teaching, and so he relocated to Capernaum on the shores of the Lake of Gennesaret. Capernaum (in the original Hebrew, Kefarnahum, "Village of Nahum") was a prosperous townlet whose inhabitants engaged mainly in fishing (a great haul of fish is recorded in Luke 5:6). Being a frontier town between the domains of Antipas and Philip, it had a customs post (the apostle Matthew may have been called from his duty there as a tax-collector; Matthew 9:9; Mark 2:3-14; Luke 5:27). A centurion commanding the local garrison, though a Gentile, had built the local synagogue (Luke 7:5), where Jesus often preached. It was at Capernaum that Jesus called his first disciples, the fishermen Simon Peter and Andrew, men of nearby Bethsaida east of the Jordan (John 1:44), as well as James and John, the sons of Zebedee; and here he invested the Twelve Apostles (Mark 3:13-19; Matthew 10:1-4). It was here also that he performed many of the miraculous deeds reported in the Gospels. From then on Capernaum was called "his own city" (Matthew 9:1). As Capernaum had a more varied population and was nearer regional and international trade routes than the remote village of Nazareth, it is likely to have been more receptive to the new teachings. Yet, Jesus did not entirely sever his ties with the region of his youth. John 2:11 continues, after the story of his baptism, with a miracle performed by Jesus at nearby Cana in the presence of Mary and the disciples. This visit to Cana occurred at the beginning of Jesus' ministry, but he is also reported to return there on a later occasion (John 4:46).

So he came again to Cana in Galilee
(John 4:46)

And he came to Nazareth where he had been brought up
(Luke 4:16)

He went to a city called Nain . . .
(Luke 7:11)

Chorazin

Capernaum

Bethsaida

Jotapata

Cana

Sepphoris

Nazareth

Exaloth

Mt. Tabor

Nain

Shunem

Magdala

Sea of Galilee

Tiberias

Sennabris

Gadora

River Jordan

0   1   2   miles
0   1   2   km.

© Carta, Jerusalem

MT. 4:12-22; 8:5-17; 9:9-10; 18-20; MK. 1:16-34; 2:1-17; 5:22-43; LK. 4:31-41; 5:27-32; 7:1-10; 8:40-56; JN. 2:1-12

Resurrection of the widow's son at Nain, Lk 7:11-17
(Painting Matthias Gerung c. 1532; Ottheinrich-Bibel, Bayerische Staatsbibliothek)

The Holy Land and Coele-Syria in the Time of Jesus

The Gospels tell that the teachings of Jesus, which mainly took place around the Sea of Galilee, drew crowds from Galilee, Judea, Jerusalem, Idumea, the lands beyond the Jordan, Tyre, and Sidon (Mark 3:7-8; Matthew 4:25 [adding "the Decapolis"] and Luke 6:17). The list of countries and towns reflects the area of Jewish settlement in the Holy Land at the time.

In Judea, Jerusalem is singled out as the only "city" proper in the land; Idumea had been a separate administrative unit since the days of Alexander Janneus, although its inhabitants were merging more and more with the rest of the Jews.

The lands "beyond the Jordan," or Perea, were Jewish from the days of the Tobiad dynasty. There were Jewish communities in the cities of the Hauran (later Decapolis) which were, however, predominantly Gentile. Finally, the territories of Tyre and Sidon, although predominantly Phoenician, had considerable Jewish populations.

Though politically split up between various territories and rulers (all of which were subject to Roman suzerainty), the Jews of the Holy Land were one spiritually and any wave of religious feeling rising in one community could sweep them all. It is significant that Samaria and the coastal cities are absent from the list, though later Christianity made much progress there.

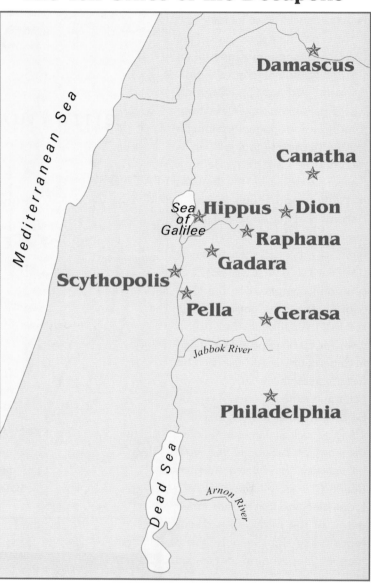

The Ten Cities of the Decapolis

Damascus

Canatha

Sea of Galilee — Hippus — Dion

Raphana

Gadara

Scythopolis

Pella — Gerasa

Jabbok River

Philadelphia

Mediterranean Sea

Dead Sea

Arnon River

	Territory of Herod Philip
	Cities under the Proconsul of Syria
	Territory of Herod Antipas
	Territory of the Procurator of Judea
....	Herod's kingdom at its greatest extent

The Four Gospels, 1495, the Evangelist dictating his Gospel
Credit: Wellcome Library, London. Wellcome Images

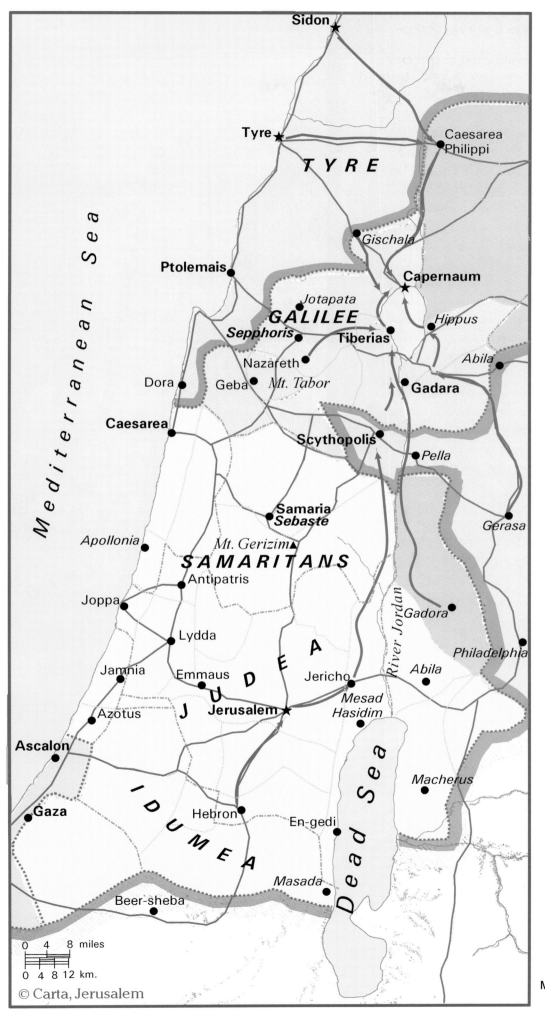

A great multitude, hearing all that he did, came to him.

(Mark 3:8)

Sidon

Tyre

TYRE

Caesarea Philippi

Mediterranean Sea

Gischala

Ptolemais

Capernaum

Jotapata

GALILEE

Hippus

Sepphoris

Tiberias

Nazareth

Abila

Dora

Geba

Mt. Tabor

Gadara

Caesarea

Scythopolis

Pella

Samaria
Sebaste

Gerasa

Apollonia

Mt. Gerizim▲

SAMARITANS

Antipatris

River Jordan

Joppa

Gadora

Lydda

J U D E A

Abila

Jamnia

Emmaus

Jericho

Philadelphia

Azotus

J

Jerusalem

Mesad Hasidim

Ascalon

I D U M E A

Macherus

Gaza

Hebron

En-gedi

Dead Sea

Masada

Beer-sheba

0 4   8 miles

0 4 8 12 km.

© Carta, Jerusalem

MT. 4:25; MK. 3:7-8; LK. 6:17

Around the Sea of Galilee

Apart from several journeys, Jesus' entire activity before his final departure for Jerusalem was concentrated around the Sea of Galilee (Matthew 15:29; Mark 1:16, 6:31), also called Lake Gennesaret (Luke 5:1) and Lake Tiberias (John 6:1, 21:1), or just "the sea" in the Gospels. The Jewish historian, Josephus Flavius, states that the local inhabitants called the body of water "the lake of Gennesaret" (War 3:463). Indeed, it seems that the name "Sea of Galilee" was coined by the early Christian community, based upon their belief that Jesus' ministry by the lake was a fulfillment of Isaiah 9:1. They derived the components for the place name from the biblical verse, the only occasion in which the terms "sea" and "Galilee" are found together.

Outside of the Gospels, Matthew, Mark and John, the name Sea of Galilee does not occur again in Jewish or pagan literature until the Byzantine era. "Sea of Tiberias" appears also in rabbinical literature and is clearly posterior to the foundation of that city in A.D. 18-19. The first Apostles were fishermen; sometimes Jesus taught while standing in a boat, with the crowds listening on the shore. The Sermon on the Mount was delivered according to tradition near Capernaum (Matthew 8:1 and 5); the site is said to be located on the height just behind Capernaum. Only occasionally did Jesus upbraid the cities that refused to repent ("Woe to you Chorazin, woe to you Bethsaida, Capernaum shall be brought down to Hades" — Matthew 11:21-23; Luke 10:13-15).

On the Sea of Galilee there are frequent storms. During one such storm, Jesus slept while sailing across the lake and upon his awakening the sea was suddenly calmed. In the only report of Jesus' travel to the lower eastern shores shores of the lake, the

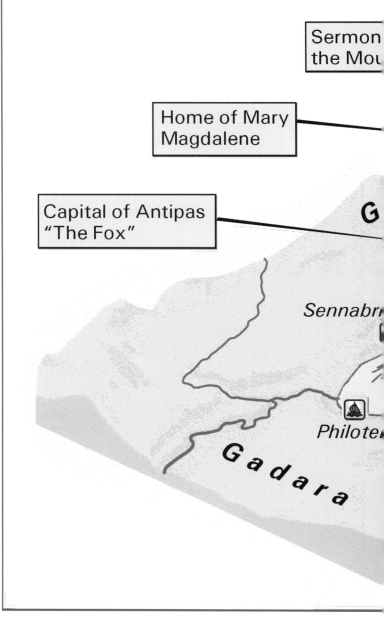

Who is this, that even wind and sea obey him?
(Mark 4:41)

Sermon
the Mou

Home of Mary
Magdalene

Capital of Antipas
"The Fox"

G

Sennabr

Philote

Gadara

Remains of an ancient boat retrieved from the Sea of Galilee
(Drawing: Carta, Jerusalem)

boat arrived near the ancient settlement of Gergesa (Mark 4:35-41; Matthew 8:23-27; Luke 8:22-24). The location of the incident of "the swine" has been much debated. Mark (5:1) and Luke (8:26, 37) describe it as "the region of the Gerasenes," while Matthew (8:28) calls it "the region of the Gadarenes." There is no history of the famous city of Gerasa, which lay nearly thirty miles south of the lake, ever possessing territory on the shores. The city of Gadara was closer, but it still lay some distance from the lake. It seems that at some point Gadara did possess a harbor on the southern end of the lake, but this location is too remote for our event. Instead, other Greek manuscripts of the New Testament event preserve the name, "the region of the Gergasenes." In ancient Jewish sources Gergesa

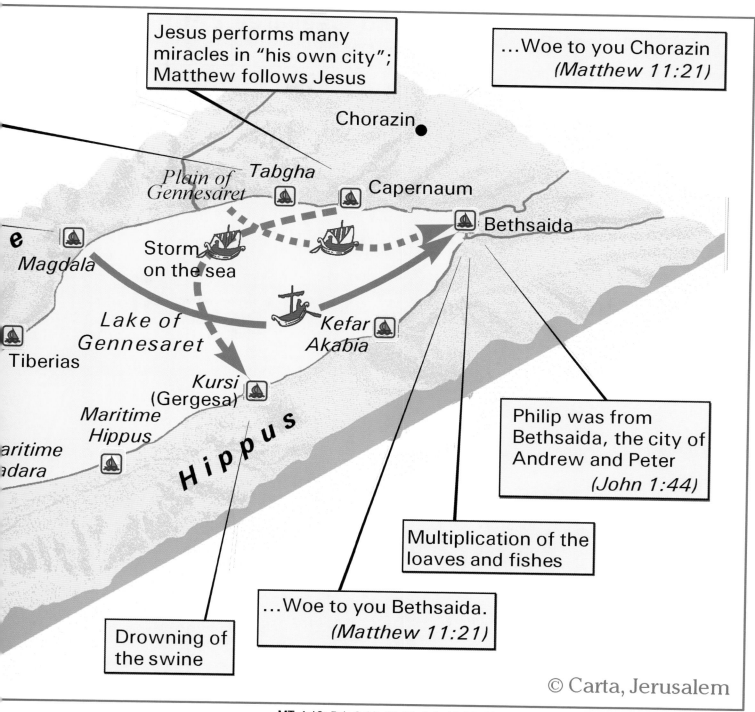

Jesus performs many miracles in "his own city"; Matthew follows Jesus

...Woe to you Chorazin (Matthew 11:21)

Chorazin

Plain of Gennesaret

Tabgha

Capernaum

Bethsaida

Magdala

Storm on the sea

Lake of Gennesaret

Kefar Akabia

Tiberias

Kursi (Gergesa)

Maritime Hippus

Maritime Gadara

Hippus

Philip was from Bethsaida, the city of Andrew and Peter (John 1:44)

Multiplication of the loaves and fishes

...Woe to you Bethsaida. (Matthew 11:21)

Drowning of the swine

© Carta, Jerusalem

MT. 4:18; 5:1; 8:18, 23-34; 9:1; 11:21; 13:1, 14:13-34; 15:29-39; MK. 2:13, 16-20; 4:1, 35-41; 5:1-21; 6:32-53; 8:1-10, 22; LK. 5:1-11; 8:22-39; 9:10-17; JN. 1:44; 6:1-25

appears as the name of a small village east of the Jordan River and is thus evidence that a village by this name existed. It seems that the confusion regarding the place name is the product of a later Greek scribal tendency to exchange the more famous city names (Gerasa or Gadara) for a city name that was unknown to them (Gergesa). In the sixth century a large monastery was founded in the area. Gergesa (Kursi) was situated on the eastern lakeshore at the base of the steep slopes in the territory of Hippus. The inhabitants of Gergesa, being Gentiles, did not share Jewish scruples regarding the raising of swine. Indeed, swine were often used for sacrifices in pagan temples (1 Maccabees 1:47).

Other events recorded in the Gospels pertaining to the Sea of Galilee and its surrounding are the Multiplication of the Loaves and Fishes in "the lonely places" near the town of Bethsaida (Luke 9:10-17), the story of Jesus walking on the water, and Peter's attempt to follow his example (Mark 6:45-51; Matthew 15:22-23; and John 6:15-21). Other journeys of Jesus include a visit to "Magadan" (Matthew 15:39; "Dalmanutha" in Mark 8:10); in both cases we should read Magdala, the most important townlet on the sea shore after Tiberias, and famous for its fishing-curing industry. This locality was the home of Mary Magdalene, who followed Jesus to Jerusalem; she was one of a group of women, "who had been healed of evil spirits and infirmities who provided for him out of their means" (Luke 8:2-3).

The Visit to Tyre, Sidon, and Caesarea Philippi

And from there he arose and went away to the region of Tyre and Sidon.
(Mark 7:24)

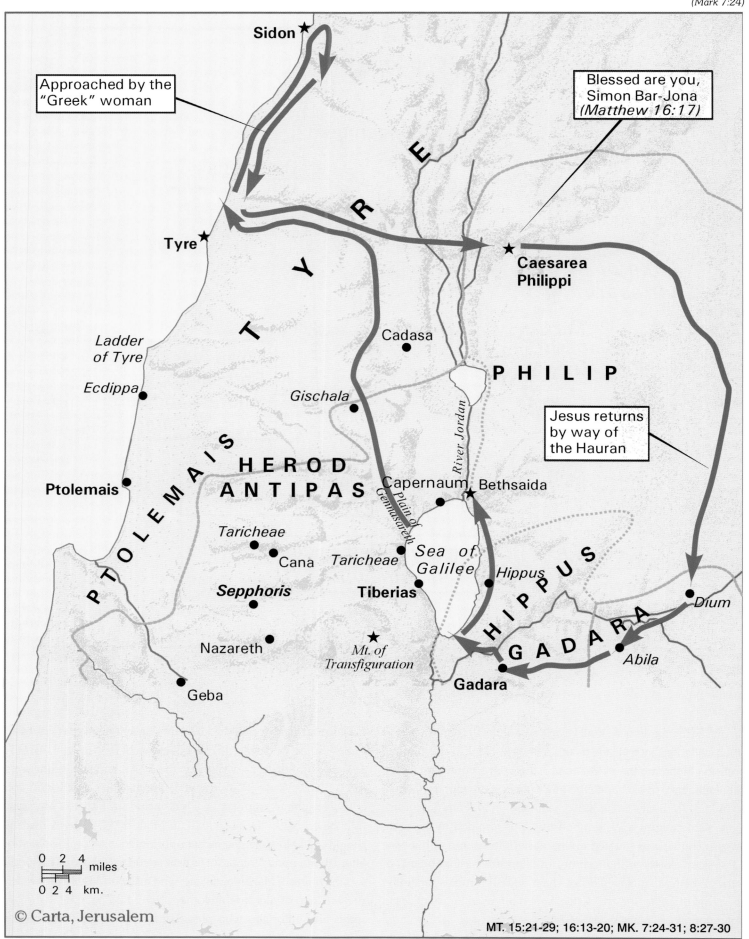

Sidon

Approached by the "Greek" woman

Blessed are you, Simon Bar-Jona *(Matthew 16:17)*

T Y R E

Tyre

Caesarea Philippi

Ladder of Tyre

Cadasa

P H I L I P

Ecdippa

Gischala

River Jordan

Jesus returns by way of the Hauran

HEROD ANTIPAS

Ptolemais

Capernaum Bethsaida

P T O L E M A I S

Taricheae

Plain of Gennasareth

Cana

Taricheae

Sea of Galilee

Hippus

H I P P U S

Sepphoris

Tiberias

Dium

G A D A R A

Nazareth

Mt. of Transfiguration

Abila

Geba

Gadara

```
0  2  4  miles
0  2  4  km.
```

© Carta, Jerusalem

MT. 15:21-29; 16:13-20; MK. 7:24-31; 8:27-30

Temple of Pan, Caesarea Philippi
(Photo: EdoM)

The only time Jesus is reported to leave the traditional boundaries of the Holy Land proper is during his journey to Tyre and Sidon. Mark 7:24 and Matthew 15:21 define this journey as one to the "region" or "district" of these two cities; we are not told whether he entered the cities themselves. Both had extensive territories; that of Sidon had a common border with the city of Damascus, far inland.

The region of Tyre reached Cadasa in the mountains overlooking the Huleh valley (Ulatha). During this journey Jesus healed the daughter of a "Greek" or "Syrophoenician" woman; that is to say, a Phoenician woman who had adopted the Hellenistic culture then common in the Roman East. According to Mark (7:31), Jesus passed through the region of the Hauran in the Transjordan (later called Decapolis) on his return to the Sea of Galilee — possibly detouring inland through Gaulanitis to the territories of Abila, Dium, Hippus and Gadara.

It is during this journey that Jesus and his disciples passed through the district of Caesarea Philippi, Hellenistic Panias, rebuilt by Herod and his son Philip. The outstanding feature of the region was the high cliffs near the city with a cave dedicated to the god Pan and many rock-cut niches holding dedicatory statues of the Nymphs. Josephus Flavius reports that Caesarea Philippi was the site of one of Herod the Great's three temples built in honor of his benefactor, Caesar Augustus (Antiquities 15:364), the others being at Caesarea on the Mediterranean and Sebaste in Samaria.

This itinerary in Matthew and Mark, but missing in Luke, may have been associated by the Evangelists with the triad of regions mentioned in Isaiah 9:1 (see Matthew 4:15): "the way of the sea (i.e. the trunk route from Tyre to Panias), the land beyond the Jordan (i.e. the Hauran/Decapolis), Galilee of the Gentiles (i.e. the return to the Galilee)."

A Phoenician woman
(On a sarcophagus from Sidon)

27

The Transfiguration

And after six days Jesus took with him Peter and James and John and led them up a high mountain ...

(Mark 9:2)

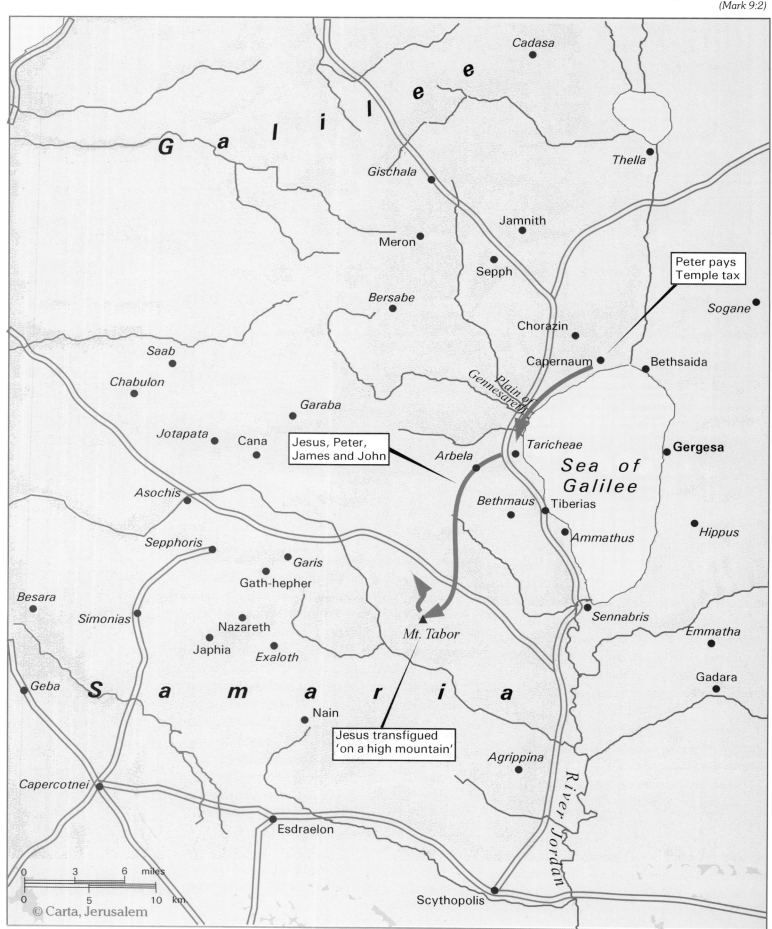

Cadasa

G a l i l e e

Thella

Gischala

Jamnith

Meron

Sepph

Bersabe

Sogane

Chorazin

Peter pays Temple tax

Saab

Capernaum

Bethsaida

Chabulon

Garaba

Plain of Gennesareth

Jotapata

Cana

Jesus, Peter, James and John

Arbela

Taricheae

Gergesa

Sea of Galilee

Asochis

Bethmaus

Tiberias

Hippus

Sepphoris

Ammathus

Garis

Gath-hepher

Besara

Simonias

Nazareth

Mt. Tabor

Sennabris

Emmatha

Japhia

Exaloth

Jesus transfigued 'on a high mountain'

Gadara

Geba

S a m a r i a

Nain

Agrippina

River Jordan

Capercotnei

0   3   6 miles

0   5   10 km

Esdraelon

Scythopolis

© Carta, Jerusalem

MT. 17:1-8; MK. 9:2-8; LK. 9:28-36

Mount of Transfiguration
(Photo: Bantosh)

In the story of Jesus' journey away from the region of the Sea of Galilee, the Gospels relate the visit of Jesus, together with the Apostles Peter, James and John, to "a high mountain" — where the Transfiguration is said to have taken place. This mountain is not named in the sources. Likely because of the mention of Caesarea Philippi in the adjoining event (Matthew 16:13-20; Mark 27:27-30), the church historian Eusebius earlier identified the slopes of Mount Hermon with the location of the Transfiguration. However, he later followed what became Christian tradition that connects the event with Mount Tabor, a prominent landmark that had served in biblical times as a boundary point between the territories of three tribes; it had been a Hellenistic fortress and later it was a Jewish one.

Subsequent to the Transfiguration Matthew tells of a significant incident at Capernaum: Jesus had Peter pay the half-shekel tax to the Temple for both of them, so as "not to give offense" (Matthew 17:24-27).

Inscription honoring Philip, son of Herod
(Drawing: Carta, Jerusalem)

Jesus' Visit to Jerusalem

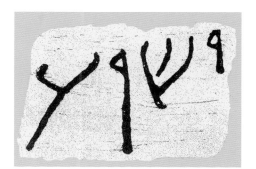

The Passover of the Jews was at hand, and Jesus went up to Jerusalem.

(John 2:13)

*The name "Jesus,"
as written in Hebrew on an ossuary*

The Gospel according to John records several more journeys of Jesus to Jerusalem, about which the other Gospels are silent. Perhaps, he continued the practice begun by his parents to travel every year to Jerusalem to celebrate the Passover (Luke 2:41). Thus in John 2:13-3:21 there is a story of a visit to Jerusalem at Passover, during which Jesus cleansed the Temple of money-changers and sellers of animals, an event placed by the other Gospels in his last days in Jerusalem (Mark 11:15-17; Matthew 21:12-13; Luke 19:45-46). According to John, it is during this stay Jesus was baptizing in Judea while John was doing the same in the well-watered plain of Aenon, near Salim (John 3:22-24). It was in the context of this ministry in Judea that Jesus passed through Samaria and met the Samaritan woman at the well of Sychar, staying two days with the Samaritans, many of whom believed in him.

One more journey to Jerusalem, during which a paralytic was healed at the pool of Bethesda in the Holy City, is recorded in John 5.

John (chapter 7) gives a slightly different version of Jesus' last journey than that found in the three other Gospels. According to John, he went secretly to Jerusalem at the Feast of Tabernacles (in the autumn); and was still there at the Feast of Dedication (i.e. Hanukkah in early winter; John 10:22), after which he returned beyond the Jordan, probably to Bethabara (John 10:40). He then came back to Bethany, raised Lazarus from the dead (John 11:46), and retired once again into the wilderness of Ephraim, northeast of Jerusalem (John 11:54).

Stairs, where Jesus may have walked leading to the Temple in Jerusalem.
(Photo: Peter van der Sluijs)

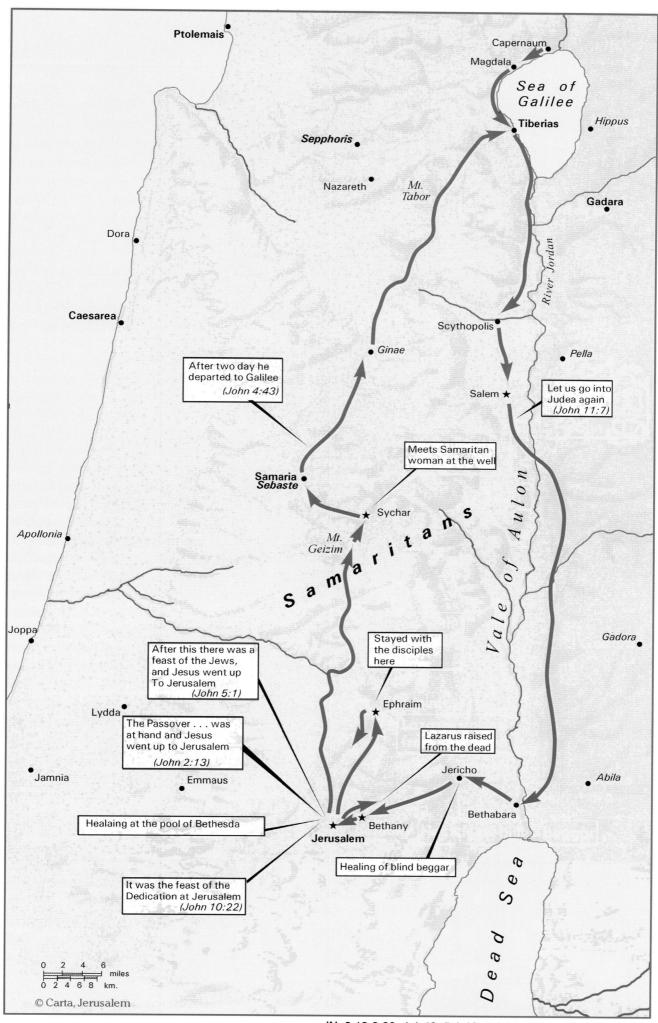

Ptolemais

Capernaum

Magdala

Sea of Galilee

Tiberias

Hippus

Sepphoris

Nazareth

Mt. Tabor

Gadara

Dora

River Jordan

Caesarea

Ginae

Scythopolis

Pella

After two day he departed to Galilee *(John 4:43)*

Salem ★

Let us go into Judea again *(John 11:7)*

Meets Samaritan woman at the well

Samaria
Sebaste

Sychar ★

Apollonia

Mt. Geizim

S a m a r i t a n s

V a l e   o f   A u l o n

Joppa

Gadora

After this there was a feast of the Jews, and Jesus went up To Jerusalem *(John 5:1)*

Stayed with the disciples here

Lydda

Ephraim ★

The Passover . . . was at hand and Jesus went up to Jerusalem *(John 2:13)*

Lazarus raised from the dead

Jericho

Abila

Jamnia

Emmaus

Bethabara

Healaing at the pool of Bethesda

★ Bethany ★

Jerusalem

Healing of blind beggar

It was the feast of the Dedication at Jerusalem *(John 10:22)*

D e a d   S e a

0   2   4   6   miles
0   2   4   6   8   km.

© Carta, Jerusalem

JN. 2:13-3:22; 4:1-42; 5:1-18; 7:1-10; 10:22, 40; 11:1-44, 54

31

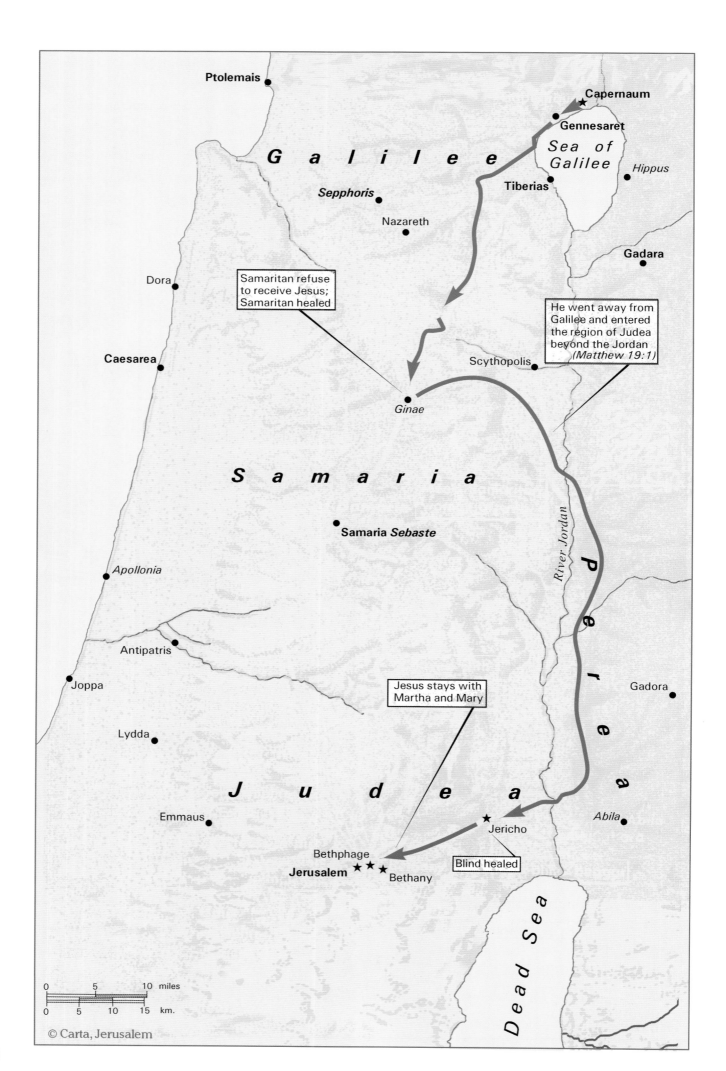

Ptolemais

Capernaum

Gennesaret

Sea of Galilee

Galilee

Hippus

Sepphoris

Nazareth

Tiberias

Gadara

Dora

Samaritan refuse
to receive Jesus;
Samaritan healed

He went away from
Galilee and entered
the region of Judea
beyond the Jordan
(Matthew 19:1)

Caesarea

Scythopolis

Ginae

Samaria

Samaria *Sebaste*

Apollonia

River Jordan

Perea

Antipatris

Joppa

Gadora

Jesus stays with
Martha and Mary

Lydda

Judea

Emmaus

Abila

Jericho

Bethphage

Blind healed

Jerusalem ★ ★ ★ Bethany

Dead Sea

0   5   10 miles
0 5 10 15 km.

© Carta, Jerusalem

Jesus' Last Journey to Jerusalem

When the days drew near for him to be received
up, he set his face to go to Jerusalem.

(Luke 9:51)

When the days drew near for him "ascent" to Jerusalem (Luke 9:51), at the end of his stay in Galilee, Jesus began to foretell of his fate in Jerusalem to his disciples, "and they were greatly distressed" (Matthew 17:23).

We may possibly insert into the story of Jesus' last journey to Jerusalem the incident mentioned in Luke 9:52-56. Perhaps Jesus intended to take the shorter route to Jerusalem by way of Samaria but, as the people would not receive him, he turned eastward and went through Perea, the "Judea beyond the Jordan." From there, he and his disciples crossed the Jordan and continued by way of Jericho, where he stayed at the house of Zacchaeus, a chief tax-collector (probably of the imperial estates in the Jordan Valley, inherited by the emperor from the Herodian dynasty). "As Jesus was leaving Jericho, he healed a blind man called Bartimaeus" (Mark 10:46-52; Matthew 20:29-34).

Then Jesus continued along the pilgrim road, which went up to the Mount of Olives and so to Bethphage on the mount and to Bethany, where he stayed at the house of Martha and Mary, the sisters of Lazarus.

Jesus, Martha and Mary; Stain-glass window in Petrópolis Cathedral.
(Photo :Eugenio Hansen)

MT. 16:21; 17:22-27; 19:1-2; 20:17, 29-34; MK.
8:31; 10:1, 32, 46-52; 11:1-2;
LK. 9:51-56; 10:38-42, 13:22; 18:31-42; 19:1-10,
28-35; JN. 12:1-8

Entrance to the Church of Bethphage, at the time of the Palm Sunday Procession.
(Photo: Ori~)

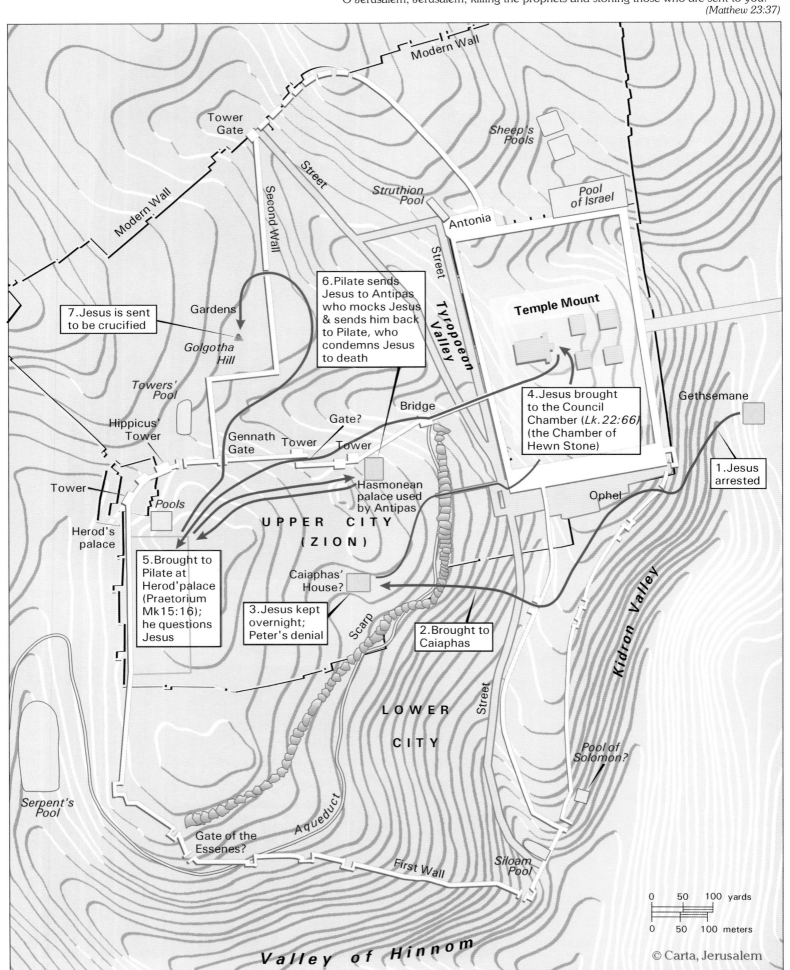

O Jerusalem, Jerusalem, killing the prophets and stoning those who are sent to you!
(Matthew 23:37)

Modern Wall

Tower Gate

Modern Wall

Second Wall

Street

Struthion Pool

Sheep's Pools

Pool of Israel

Antonia

Temple Mount

7. Jesus is sent to be crucified

Gardens

6. Pilate sends Jesus to Antipas who mocks Jesus & sends him back to Pilate, who condemns Jesus to death

Golgotha Hill

Tyropoeon Valley

4. Jesus brought to the Council Chamber (*Lk. 22:66*) (the Chamber of Hewn Stone)

Gethsemane

Towers' Pool

Bridge

Hippicus' Tower

Gate?

Gennath Gate

Tower

Tower

Tower

Pools

Hasmonean palace used by Antipas

1. Jesus arrested

Ophel

Herod's palace

5. Brought to Pilate at Herod' palace (Praetorium Mk 15:16); he questions Jesus

UPPER CITY (ZION)

Caiaphas' House?

3. Jesus kept overnight; Peter's denial

Scarp

2. Brought to Caiaphas

Kidron Valley

LOWER CITY

Street

Serpent's Pool

Pool of Solomon?

Aqueduct

Gate of the Essenes?

First Wall

Siloam Pool

0 50 100 yards

0 50 100 meters

Valley of Hinnom

© Carta, Jerusalem

MT. 21-27; MK. 11-15; LK. 19:28-23:56; JN. 12-19

Jesus' Trial, Judgment and Crucifixion

On his last visit to Jerusalem, Jesus resided in Bethany on the eastern slopes of the Mount of Olives. His initial approach to the city, which is invariably referred to as the Triumphal Entry, brought him on the colt of a she-ass found at a village opposite Bethphage.

As he neared the Holy City, he was greeted with the traditional blessing given to pilgrims citing Psalm 118:26, "Blessed is he who comes in the name of the Lord." The pilgrim typically responded from the second half of the same verse, "We bless you from the house of the Lord." The Synoptic Gospels record the cleansing of the temple of the money-changers on this visit to Jerusalem (Matthew 21:12-13; Mark 11:15-17; Luke 19:45-46). Later that week Jesus and his entourage from Galilee celebrated the Passover Seder in a large upper room, "furnished and ready" (Mark 14:15 and Luke 22:12), of a house within the walled city of Jerusalem, in accordance with contemporary Jewish requirements. We may assume that it took place in the wealthy Upper City of Jerusalem, at the home of one who was well-familiar with Jesus. After the meal, Jesus and the disciples descended to the Kidron Valley, to Gethsemane ("the Oil Press") at the foot of the Mount of Olives. There he was arrested by a crowd armed with swords and clubs, led by Judas Iscariot, one of the Twelve, who had betrayed his master.

According to the Gospels Jesus was led to the house of the high priest Caiaphas, there to be interrogated first by the former high priest Annas and other leaders of the Temple establishment. It was during these events that Peter, who was waiting outside in the courtyard of the palatial home, thrice denied Jesus.

Church of the Flaggelation, Jerusalem
Author: ReeveJ

THE VIA DOLOROSA, FROM THE OMARIYA SCHOOL TO THE CHURCH OF THE HOLY SEPULCHRE

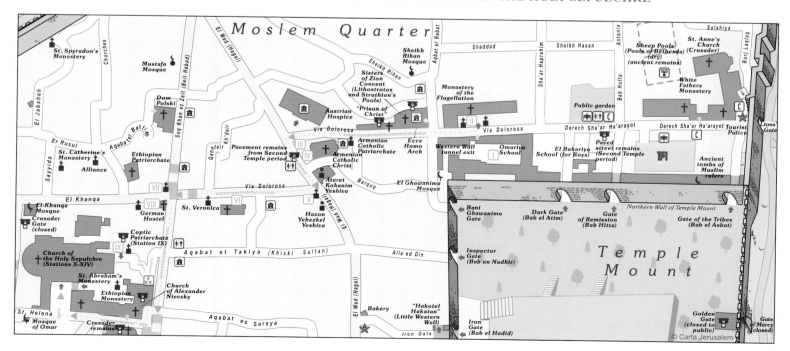

And they found the stone rolled away from the tomb, but when they went in they did not find the body.

(Luke 24:2-3)

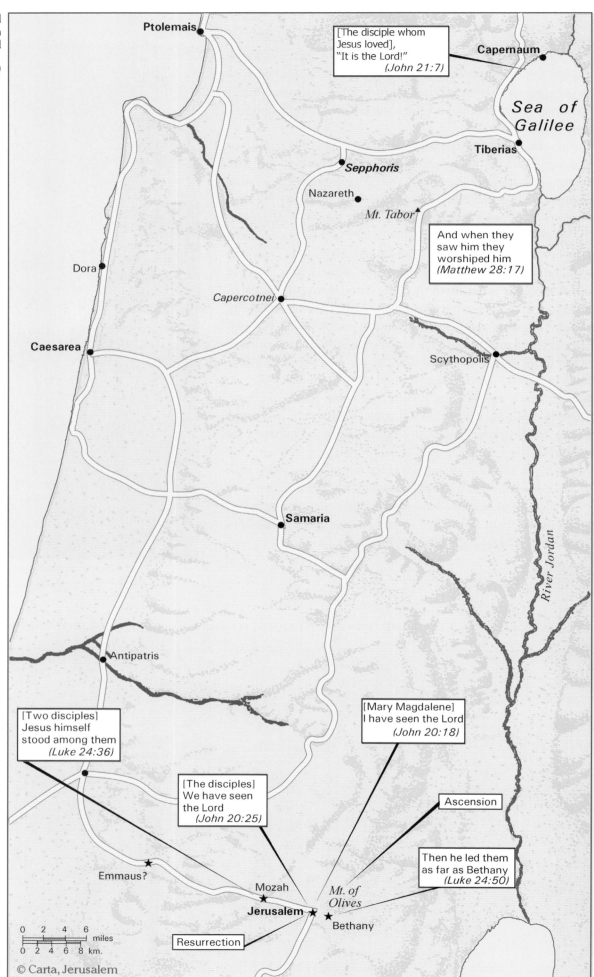

[The disciple whom Jesus loved], "It is the Lord!" *(John 21:7)*

Capernaum

Sea of Galilee

Ptolemais

Tiberias

Sepphoris

Nazareth

Mt. Tabor

And when they saw him they worshiped him *(Matthew 28:17)*

Dora

Capercotnei

Caesarea

Scythopolis

River Jordan

Samaria

Antipatris

[Mary Magdalene] I have seen the Lord *(John 20:18)*

[Two disciples] Jesus himself stood among them *(Luke 24:36)*

[The disciples] We have seen the Lord *(John 20:25)*

Ascension

Then he led them as far as Bethany *(Luke 24:50)*

Emmaus?

Mozah

Mt. of Olives

Jerusalem

Bethany

Resurrection

0 2 4 6 miles
0 2 4 6 8 km.

© Carta, Jerusalem

MT. 28; MK. 16; LK. 24; JN. 20-21; ACTS 1:2-12; 1 COR. 15:7

The Resurrection and Ascension

The Gospels are unanimous in continuing the story of Jesus after the Crucifixion. According to Christian belief, Jesus rose from the dead on the third day after his crucifixion. The Gospels record appearances of the risen Christ in Galilee (Matthew and Mark) and in Judea, at Emmaus (possibly Mozah), Bethany, Jerusalem (John, Luke and Matthew by inference). Finally, we are told (Acts 1:2-12), he ascended to heaven from the Mount of Olives.

Diptych with Scenes of Jesus's Life and Passion, late 14th century
(Acquired by Henry Walters, 1922)

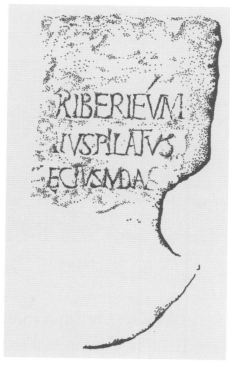

Inscription of Pontius Pilate,
found at Caesarea
(Drawing: Carta, Jerusalem)

Herod's family tomb with the rolling stone,
Jerusalem
(Photo:Alistair from Montreal, Canada)

Ancient olive trees in the Garden of Gethsemane
(Photo: Chad Rosentha)l

The Church in the First Century A.D.

The Forum at Philippi
(Author:Carole Raddato, from Frankfurt, Germany)

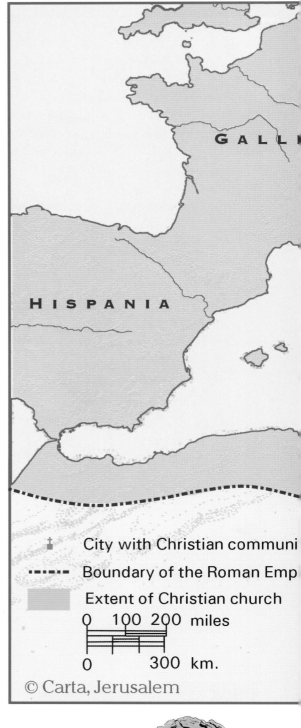

GALLI

HISPANIA

✝ City with Christian communi

------ Boundary of the Roman Emp

Extent of Christian church

0   100 200   miles

0   300 km.

© Carta, Jerusalem

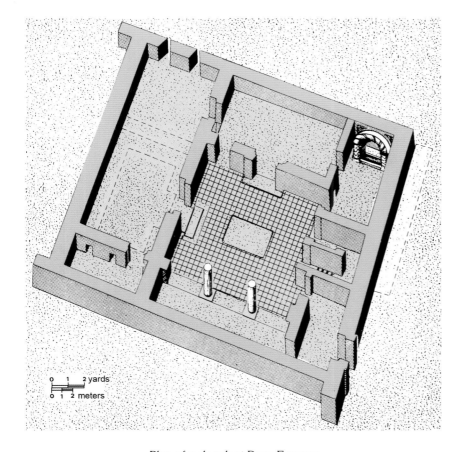

0 1 2 yards
0 1 2 meters

Plan of a church at Dura-Europos
(Drawing: Carta, Jerusalem)

Nero Caesar
(Drawing: Carta,
Jerusalem)

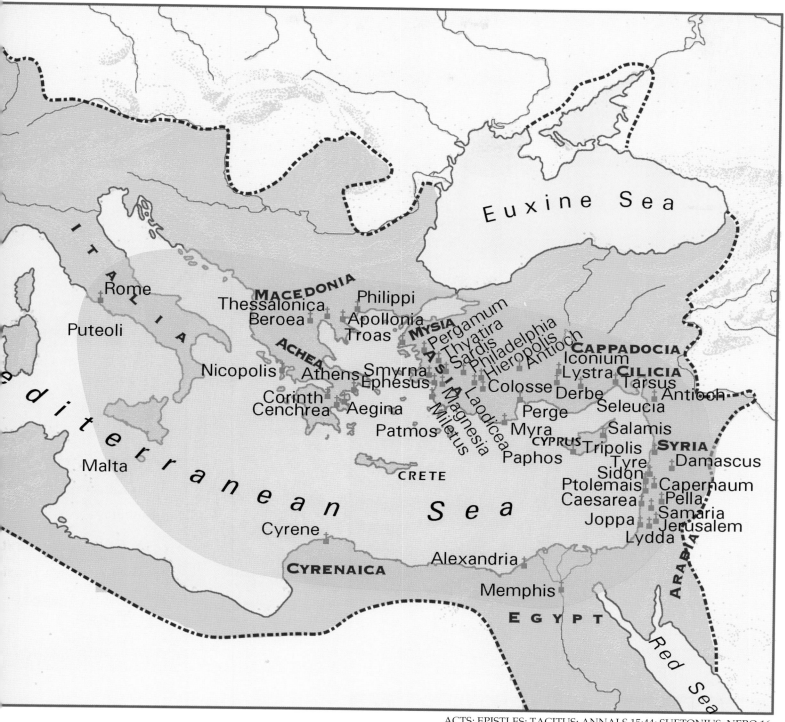

I hope to see you passing as I go to Spain.
(Romans 15:24)

ACTS; EPISTLES; TACITUS: ANNALS 15:44; SUETONIUS: NERO 16

The geographical distribution of Christian communities in the Roman Empire in this century reflects the missionary activities of Paul and his fellow Apostles, based on the network of synagogues in the Jewish diaspora. Born as Jews, they were freely admitted to the synagogues, where their teachings often provoked dissension and split the local community; but almost always there remained, after the expulsion or departure of the Apostles themselves, a small group of Christians perpetuating the existence of the Church. These scattered communities were assiduously nursed by Paul and his representatives, as is evident from the Apostle's letters.

Gradually the missionary teachings attracted a growing number of Gentiles, among whom the Judeo-Christians were gradually absorbed. Apart from Edessa beyond the Euphrates, the Church of the first century A.D. was restricted to the Roman Empire. Apparently most of the early Christians were concentrated in Asia Minor, where the Jewish communities had long been established and had created around them a circle of half-proselytized "God-fearing" Gentiles. It was in these circles that the Christian message based upon a reinterpretation of the venerated Old Testament took root. In the West only Rome and its vicinity, and possibly also Spain, had Christian communities at this early stage. The first persecution (under Nero) was short and did not hinder the growth of the Church.

Places Visited by Jesus

After this, Jesus traveled about from one town and village to another, proclaiming the good news of the kingdom of God.

(Luke 8:1)

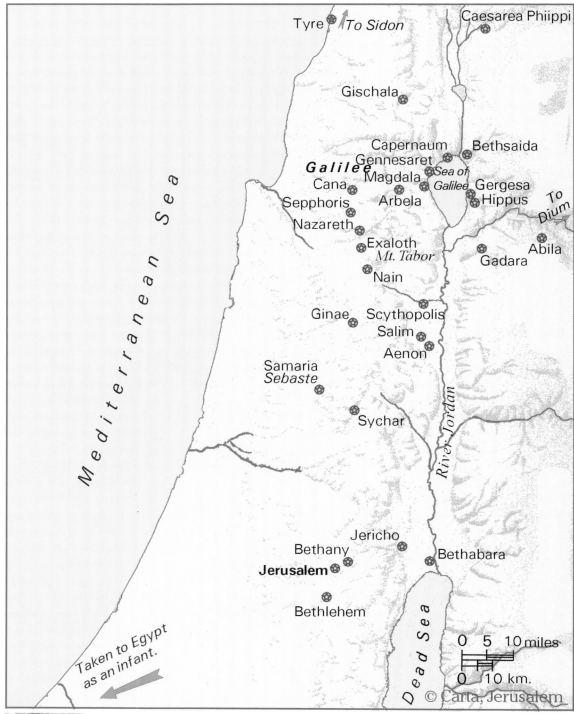

Tyre
To Sidon
Caesarea Phiippi
Gischala
Capernaum
Bethsaida
Galilee
Gennesaret
Magdala
Sea of Galilee
Cana
Arbela
Gergesa
Hippus
To Dium
Sepphoris
Nazareth
Exaloth
Mt. Tabor
Gadara
Abila
Nain
Ginae
Scythopolis
Salim
Aenon
Samaria
Sebaste
Sychar
River Jordan
Jericho
Bethany
Bethabara
Jerusalem
Bethlehem
Dead Sea

Mediterranean Sea

Taken to Egypt as an infant.

0 5 10 miles
0 10 km.

© Carta, Jerusalem

Title: Life of Jesus.
Anonymous artist (ca.1497-1500)
National Museum in Warsaw
Source/Photographer Web Gallery of Art